Study Guide for
Let Nobody Turn Us Around

Study Guide for
Let Nobody Turn Us Around

Andrea Queeley

ROWMAN & LITTLEFIELD PUBLISHERS, INC.
Lanham • Boulder • New York • Oxford

ROWMAN & LITTLEFIELD PUBLISHERS, INC.

Published in the United States of America
by Rowman & Littlefield Publishers, Inc.
A Member of the Rowman & Littlefield Publishing Group
4501 Forbes Boulevard, Suite 200, Lanham, Maryland 20706
www.rowmanlittlefield.com

P.O. Box 317, Oxford OX2 9RU, United Kingdom

British Library Cataloguing in Publication Information Available

Library of Congress Cataloging-in-Publication Data
Queeley, Andrea.
    Study guide for Let nobody turn us around / Andrea Queeley.
        p.   cm.
    ISBN 0-7425-2709-3 (pkb. : alk. paper)
    1. Let nobody turn us around—Examinations—Study guides.   2. African
Americans—History—Examinations—Study guides.   3. African
Americans—Civil rights—History—Examinations—Study guides.   4.
African Americans—Social conditions—Examinations—Study guides.   I.
Title.
E184.6.L4837   2003
973'.0496073—dc21   2003003691

Printed in the United States of America

∞ ™ The paper used in this publication meets the minimum requirements
of American National Standard for Information Sciences—Permanence of
Paper for Printed Library Materials, ANSI/NISO Z39.48-1992.

Contents

Introduction to the Study Guide

*L*et Nobody Turn Us Around: Voices of Resistance, Reform, and Renewal provides students with a collection of readings that capture the main ideological currents of the Black Freedom Movement in the United States from 1789 to the present. Each section begins with an introductory essay to frame the ideas and activism of the period under consideration. While each document contains a preface that situates the text and its author in the context of the political activism of the time, the documents themselves are meant to inform readers about the theoretical underpinnings of the activism rather than the particular movements themselves.

This study guide is designed to complement each section of the book. Key Points, summaries of the section introductions, highlight the main points and thus offer guidance for lecture preparation. Following these summaries, Comprehension and Thought Questions address each individual document appearing in the section. These questions range in difficulty and are aimed at ensuring that the student recognizes key factual aspects of the document or its author; the questions address the significant ideas and features. They can be answered without the use of outside sources and many require that the student reflect upon her own experiences or opinions.

Essay Questions that address major themes are provided for the introduction and each of the five sections. Ideal for use in exams or homework assignments, these questions require the student to draw upon several readings in the section, incorporate the information presented, and use it to form a coherent response. While students can utilize substantiated knowledge from outside of the text, the documents should be the basis upon which students' responses are formulated. The Essay Questions provide instructors with an opportunity to assess student reading comprehension as well as analytical skills. Some of the questions might also form the basis for classroom discussion.

Suggested Research Topics follow the Essay Questions; they are derived from the themes and issues of the section. The topics suggest areas of investigation that would be ideal for more comprehensive student projects requiring considerable outside research. The items are meant to be fairly general to allow the student to choose an aspect of the topic that he wishes to research in depth, exercising creativity and motivation. The section Classroom Exercises suggests activities aimed at fostering student engagement with the subject through interaction with the instructor and other students. Instructors are encouraged to tailor these exercises to fit the needs of their particular classroom environment.

The final feature of the study guide, Media and Internet Resources, is a list of films and websites that are relevant to each section. The films are ideal for classroom viewing and discussion. The websites provide an additional teaching and learning tool for teachers and students who wish to enhance their understanding of the themes and topics of the Black Freedom Movement presented in *Let Nobody Turn Us Around.*

Introduction

Resistance, Reform, and Renewal in the Black Experience

KEY POINTS

- **African Americans' historical depth.** Africans brought to and enslaved in North America came with individual and group histories. The authors emphasize the agency of African Americans both within the institution of slavery and after its demise through pointing to their struggle for equality.
- **Integrationism and Black Nationalism** are the two opposing ideologies that emerged during the debate over the abolition of slavery. A third perspective that emerged from labor activism is identified as **Transformationism.** Though the roots of transformationism extend back into the nineteenth century (exemplified by figures such as Nat Turner and Henry Highland Garnett, who sought to dismantle structures of oppression), Black radicalism as an ideological position solidified with the development of the Black working class in the twentieth century.
- **Race, Class, and Gender** have been central to theorizing African American liberation. Black women activists have been at the forefront of this conceptualization.
- **Theory.** This book's emphasis is on the *theory* that has informed social movements rather than on the movements themselves. Students are encouraged to connect the theoretical claims put forth in the works in this volume to social movements.

3

ESSAY QUESTIONS

1. What do you think are the strengths and weaknesses of integrationism, Black Nationalism, and transformationalism?
2. Identify at least three organizations or public figures that subscribe to each ideology (nine total). Organizations and figures can be from the past or contemporary period. Briefly explain why you think that they adhere to an integrationist, Black Nationalist, or transformationalist ideology.
3. Why do you think that race, class, and gender have been central to theorizing African American liberation and that Black women have been leaders in this way of theorizing?

CLASSROOM EXERCISES

1. Divide the classroom into teams and have a formal debate with each team representing opposing ideologies.
2. Have students write answers to the following questions and share their responses with the class:
3. How does race, gender, and class affect people's lives? How has it affected your life?

Section One

Foundations

Slavery and Abolitionism, 1789–1861

KEY POINTS

- **Racism historically constructed.** The belief in the innate inferiority of people of African descent was developed and accepted over time in the context of chattel slavery. This suggests that racism is a historically constructed social phenomenon rather than a biological and therefore natural occurrence between inherently inferior and superior groups.
- **Resistance.** Different groups of people of African descent resisted the institution of slavery by various means. Resistance is overt collective action designed for an immediate end to a specific form of repression.
- **Reform.** There were also different strategies of reform. One strategy was to enlist the assistance of White sympathizers and another was to link the anti-slavery movement to other struggles of the time. Reform is long-term gradual change based on dialogue and reconciliation.
- **Renewal.** The renewal of communities came through the affirmation of bonds of family, community, and humanity. It refers to the efforts by a group (such as fostering institutions to provide goods and services) to ensure its own survival and sustainability. The church was the most important institution in this process.

- **Solidarity.** The creation of a "Black world" of social institutions was based on the appeal to racial solidarity and collective self-help. This could not have been achieved without a belief in the existence of a global kinship among people of African descent and in the interconnectedness of their fate.

COMPREHENSION AND THOUGHT QUESTIONS

1. "The Interesting Narrative of the Life of Olaudah Equiano," Olaudah Equiano, 1789
   a. In what century did Olaudah Equiano live?
   b. How old was he when he was sold into slavery?
   c. Name three of the things he experienced during the Middle Passage.
   d. What was the first place in the Americas that he landed?
   e. In Equiano's narrative, he mentions slavery being part of life in his homeland of eastern Nigeria. Do you think the experiences of slavery in Africa differed from those in the Americas? How and why?
2. "Thus Doth Ethiopia Stretch Forth Her Hand from Slavery . . . ," Prince Hall, 1797
   a. What organization did Prince Hall help to initiate?
   b. In what other movement was he involved?
   c. Hall makes reference to conditions in the West Indies. How do you think he was informed of slavery in other parts of the Americas and what was the importance of knowing about what was happening outside of North America?
3. The Founding of the African Methodist Episcopal Church, Richard Allen, 1816
   a. What social institution did Richard Allen help to found?
   b. What incident led Allen to found this institution?
   c. How does the exclusion of African Americans from European American religious institutions relate to the integrationism vs. Black Nationalism debate?
4. David Walker's "Appeal," 1829–1830
   a. To what African American newspaper did David Walker contribute?

    b. What kind of tactics did he encourage enslaved African Americans to employ in order to achieve liberation?

    c. On what does David Walker blame the suffering of people of African descent?

    d. What are the hypocrisies that Walker points to in this appeal? Why do you think that he points out such contradictions?

    e. Throughout his narrative, Walker uses innumerable explanations and appears to be very agitated. Why is David Walker so angry?

5. The Statement of Nat Turner, 1831

    a. How many years before the outbreak of the Civil War did Nat Turner lead a slave revolt?

    b. How many people participated in this rebellion?

    c. Who wrote Turner's confessions?

    d. Why did people say that Nat Turner would be a prophet?

    e. Why did Nat Turner return to the plantation that he had run away from?

    f. In this document, Turner is recorded as receiving spiritual guidance throughout his life. How is the relationship between resistance and spirituality evidenced in his story? What do you think about the relationship between religion or spirituality and social change?

    g. What were the specific reasons Turner gives for his revolt?

    h. When the interviewer asks Turner if he is sorry for his violent actions, how does he respond?

6. Slaves Are Prohibited to Read and Write by Law

    a. What were the punishments for educating a slave?

    b. The punishment for teaching a slave to read, write, and perform mathematical calculations is different for a White person, a free "colored" person and a slave. What do the differences tell you about the social structure of slave society?

    c. Why were slave owners so concerned about slaves being educated?

7. "What if I Am a Woman?" Maria W. Stewart, 1833

    a. To what areas of social activism were women limited?

    b. According to Stewart, what would allow the man of color to be as successful as White men?

    c. What does she implore people to do in order to improve their condition?

   d. By calling for heightened moral standards in the Black community, is Stewart laying the responsibility for the Black condition on Black people themselves? Explain.

8. A Slave Denied the Rights to Marry, Letter of Milo Thompson, Slave, 1834
   a. From reading this document, what attitude did White slaveholders appear to have about their slaves getting married?
   b. Do you think slaveholding Whites viewed Blacks primarily as their property, as human beings, or as both? Explain.
   c. What were the consequences of the slaveholders' attitudes and practices about slave marriages on the enslaved?
   d. What impact do you think that the form of coercion described in this section had on individuals and communities?

9. The Selling of Slaves, Advertisement, 1835
   a. When was the transatlantic slave trade technically outlawed?
   b. What was the legal status of a slave?
   c. What could slaves be exchanged for?
   d. What elements of the descriptions of enslaved people in the advertisements strike you? What do they reveal about the African American population?

10. Solomon Northrup Describes a New Orleans Slave Auction, 1841
    a. How did Solomon Northrup become a slave?
    b. What was the name of his narrative?
    c. What would hurt the sale of a slave?
    d. How do you think the auction block experience described in this section impacted African Americans? How did reading this impact you?

11. Cinque and the *Amistad* Revolt, 1841
    a. Where was the ship *Amistad* headed at the time of the revolt?
    b. Where in the United States did *Amistad* land?
    c. On what basis did the Supreme Court rule to free the Africans of *Amistad*?
    d. What does this case reveal about the difference between a "kidnapped African" and a slave?

12. "Let Your Motto Be Resistance!" Henry Highland Garnett, 1843
    a. By what means did Garnett advocate for the overthrow of the system of slavery?
    b. What president did Garnett advise?
    c. What was his alternative to seeking racial justice in the United States?
    d. Where did Garnett die?
    e. Why do you think that Garnett talked about the American Revolution in this argument for the overthrow of slavery?
    f. How did Garnett's religious beliefs influence his argument against slavery?

13. "Slavery as It Is," William Wells Brown, 1847
    a. How many times did Brown try to escape slavery?
    b. In what social reform movements was he a leader?
    c. Name three of his works.
    d. What do you think was the effect of discussing how Europeans have responded to the contradiction between American slavery and democracy?

14. "A'n't I a Woman?" Sojourner Truth, 1851
    a. Sojourner Truth is considered to be the foremother of what ideology?
    b. How did Sojourner Truth come to be free?
    c. From the two versions of Truth's speech, identify her arguments for the rights of women and African Americans. Why do you think that she didn't contest the idea that women and Black people had less "intellect" than White men?
    d. How did "Sojourner" acquire her name and what did her name signify?
    e. How do you think an audience of White women felt about Sojourner Truth's arguments about women and gender?
    f. What did the phrase "A'n't I a Woman?" convey to White women sitting in the audience listening to Sojourner Truth?

15. A Black Nationalist Manifesto, Martin R. Delany, 1852
    a. Of what political ideology was Martin Delany a major architect?
    b. Over what did he and Frederick Douglass differ?

    c. What did Delany advocate in order to elevate people of color?

    d. What does this document reveal about the role of gender in the oppression and liberation of African Americans according to Delany?

    e. Did Delany believe that Black people have a future in the United States? Why or why not?

16. "What to the Slave Is the Fourth of July?" Frederick Douglass, 1852

    a. Why do you think that White abolitionists invited Douglass to speak at the Fourth of July celebration?

    b. Douglass describes the celebration of the Fourth of July and, by implication, American democracy as hypocritical. What reasons does he give for his criticism of American political institutions?

    c. Why did Douglass write *Narrative of the Life of Frederick Douglass?*

    d. In what reform movements was Douglass involved?

    e. Where did Douglass live outside of the United States?

    f. Does Douglass reject American democracy or does he want to be included within it? Explain your answer using the text.

    g. Do you think that Douglass's arguments against the celebration of the Fourth of July are relevant in contemporary U.S. society? Why or why not?

17. The Dred Scott Case and Its Aftermath

    a. Who was Dred Scott?

    b. On what basis did Scott win his suit? On what basis was this victory overruled?

    c. What is the role of race in the court's decision to deny Dred Scott his freedom?

    d. Why did Chief Justice Taney state that the Negro has "no rights that the White man is bound to respect"?

18. "Whenever the Colored Man Is Elevated . . . ," John Rock, 1858

    a. John Rock was the first African American to do what?

    b. Against what claim about the Black man does Rock argue?

    c. Why do you think that Rock incorporates a comparison of White and Black physical appearance in his speech?

19. The Spirituals: "Go Down, Moses" and "Didn't My Lord Deliver Daniel"
    a. What roles did spirituals play in the lives of the enslaved?
    b. Do you think that Christianity was a positive or negative force in the lives of African Americans during slavery? Why or why not?
    c. Based on the lyrics of the spirituals, what differences seem to exist between White Christianity and the religion in the enslaved community?
    d. Many spirituals emphasize images from the Old Testament, especially the story of Exodus. Why did the Exodus story have an impact upon African Americans?

ESSAY QUESTIONS

1. How are the themes of resistance, reform, and renewal evidenced in this section? Draw examples from at least ten of the nineteen excerpts.
2. The authors state in the introduction that slave narratives were a mechanism by which Whites were swayed to sympathize with the abolition movement. What parts in Olaudah Equiano's narrative would encourage late-eighteenth-century European Americans to join the movement and why?
3. Based on the excerpts in this section, describe the day-to-day experience of slavery. How was this experience different for men and women, people born in Africa and those born in America, and children and adults?
4. Identify evidence of the relationship between the anti-slavery movement and religion. What role did religion play in African Americans' struggle to end slavery?
5. Compare and contrast the cases of Dred Scott and *Amistad.* What do these cases reveal about race, nationality, and the U.S. legal system?
6. Drawing from the commentary in this section, identify and explain the grounds upon which African Americans argued for the destruction of the institution of slavery.

SUGGESTED RESEARCH TOPICS

1. The lives, work, and activism of free African Americans in the eighteenth and nineteenth centuries

2. The Church in the African American community
3. The historical trajectory of the Back-to-Africa Movement
4. Slave resistance in the Americas
5. Black women and social activism

CLASSROOM EXERCISES

1. Choose one of the trials mentioned in this section (that of Nat Turner, Dred Scott, or the freedom fighters of *Amistad*) and stage a reenactment. Students must become familiar with and articulate the key issues that concern the case and its historical significance for the African American struggle.
2. Have students choose a Biblical story, interpret it from the vantage point of an enslaved person, and share their interpretation with the class.

MEDIA AND INTERNET RESOURCES

Films

Amistad, Sankofa, The Middle Passage (HBO), Africans in America Series (PBS, 1998), *Glory, Roots, Burn! Mandingo, The Massachusetts 59*[th] *Colored Infantry* (PBS, 1991), The Civil War Series (PBS, Ken Burns, 1989), *Roots of Resistance* (PBS, 1989)

Websites

Africans in America
    www.pbs.org/wgbh/aia/home.html
American Slave Narratives: An Online Anthology
    xroads.virginia.edu/~hyper/wpa.wpahome.html
Abolitionism 1830–1850
    www.iath.virginia.edu/utc/abolitn/abhp.html
The Underground Railroad
    www.nationalgeographic.com/features/00/railroad/!1.html
The Church in the Southern Black Community
    docsouth.unc.edu/church

Section Two

Reconstruction and Reaction

The Aftermath of Slavery and the Dawn of Segregation, 1861–1915

KEY POINTS

- Referring to the period immediately following the Civil War, the Reconstruction era was a period in which African Americans and their White allies struggled to extend full democratic rights to Black people in the United States. This included fighting not only for democratic participation in government through universal male suffrage and holding political office, but also for the basic educational skills and economic resources needed to transform the conditions of the formerly enslaved.
- In this concerted effort to take advantage of the opening that the Northern victory and abolition offered, African Americans fought against reactionaries who succeeded in eroding their political and civil rights. With the Compromise of 1877 in which federal troops were withdrawn from the South, African Americans were left to the mercy of former slave owners. Black people were eliminated from state legislatures, ejected from the U.S. Congress, trapped in the sharecropping system which often degenerated into debt peonage, excluded from public accommodations, residentially segregated, denied access to education and other essential services, denied the protection of the justice system, and terrorized by racist White mobs.
- Two major responses to the institutionalization of Jim Crow segregation were the strategies of political accommodation and

13

self-help represented by Booker T. Washington's Tuskegee Machine and liberal integrationist militancy reflected in the National Association for the Advancement of Colored People (NAACP), led by W. E. B. Du Bois.

- Carrying on the legacy of resistance to racial and gender oppression, women of African descent established local associations that promoted racial uplift and addressed women's rights. Black women were in the forefront of the anti-lynching campaign, the effort to end the convict-leasing system, and the repeal of Jim Crow car laws.

- African American workers organized the Colored National Labor Union and efforts were made to encourage Black people to join workers' movements due to the severe economic exploitation that they suffered. However, racism was a significant barrier to constructing multi-racial trade unions and the development of a movement that bridged the political divide between a race-conscious movement and the class struggle of workers' movements.

COMPREHENSION AND THOUGHT QUESTIONS

1. "What the Black Man Wants," Frederick Douglass, 1865
   a. Who is Douglass's audience in this document?
   b. How does Douglass define freedom and why?
   c. What does Douglass advocate is needed in order to actualize true freedom?
   d. What reasons does Douglass give for extending suffrage to Black men?
   e. Explain the relationship Douglass makes between the notion of racial inferiority and oppression.
2. Henry McNeal Turner, Black Christian Nationalist
   a. Within what institutions did Turner rise to leadership and prominence?
   b. Who appointed Turner the first Black U.S. Army Chaplain?
   c. To whom and under what circumstances does Turner make this address?
   d. What is Turner protesting?
3. Black Urban Workers during Reconstruction
   a. Why did large numbers of African Americans migrate to the North after the Civil War?

    b. Why were labor conditions in the North difficult?

    c. What city contained the largest proportion of skilled African American labor in the United States in 1870? How did this come about?

    d. What was the role of the trades union in the experience of African American workers?

    e. How did the skilled laborers respond to labor conditions in Maryland?

4. Frances Ellen Watkins Harper, Pioneering Black Feminist

    a. Identify two published works by Frances Ellen Watkins Harper.

    b. What is the role of women in human advancement according to Harper?

    c. What does she propose needs to occur to improve the nation?

    d. Did Harper support universal suffrage? Why or why not?

5. "Labor and Capital Are in Deadly Conflict," T. Thomas Fortune, 1886

    a. What nineteenth-century philosopher and political economist was a great influence on Fortune?

    b. What evidence does Fortune present to support the claim that labor and capital are in deadly conflict?

    c. Does Fortune suggest a resolution to this conflict? If so, what does he suggest?

6. Edward Wilmot Blyden and the African Diaspora

    a. Describe the theory of Pan-Africanism. How is this theory in evidence in Blyden's personal history?

    b. What text does Blyden use to interpret world events and conditions?

    c. What problems did abolitionists and colonists address?

    d. What are the three phases of "the Negro problem" according to Blyden?

    e. What similarities and differences exist between European and African American colonists?

7. "The Democratic Idea Is Humanity," Alexander Crummell, 1888

    a. In which three countries did Crummell live?

    b. To whom was he mentor?

    c. What organization did he establish in 1897?

    d. What is Crummell's understanding of race and how does

    this understanding support his argument for the civil and political equality of all peoples?

8. "A Voice From the South," Anna Julia Cooper, 1892
   a. In what institutions was Anna Julia Cooper educated?
   b. What is the significance of her 1892 book, "A Voice From the South"?
   c. According to Cooper, what is the role that women must play in American society?
   d. What racial differences does she observe in the area of gender relations?

9. The National Association of Colored Women: Mary Church Terrell and Josephine St. Pierre Ruffin
   a. What attributes does Mary Church Terrell ascribe to women of African descent and against what accusations is she defending them?
   b. What profession did women dominate? What significance does this have to the progress of the race?
   c. In what social issues were women of African descent involved?
   d. How does Ruffin characterize the relationship between Northern and Southern White women in the post–Civil War South?
   e. How does Ruffin represent the formerly enslaved population and how does this compare with Terrell's representation?

10. "I Know Why the Caged Bird Sings," Paul Laurence Dunbar
    a. Why do you think that Dunbar was best known for his "dialect poetry"?
    b. Choose one of the three poems in this section and explain how its message is relevant to the circumstances that people of African descent confronted during the era under consideration in this section.

11. Booker T. Washington and the Politics of Accommodation
    a. What institution did Washington found and why was it significant?
    b. What did Washington promote to be the solution to the "Negro problem"?
    c. How would you characterize Washington's representation of people of African descent in his Atlanta Exposition address? What are the advantages and disadvantages of this characterization?

d. According to Washington, what are the merits of industrial education?

e. What is the relationship between the political disenfranchisement of Black men after Reconstruction and the rise of industrial education?

f. What were Washington's arguments against legal segregation?

12. William Monroe Trotter and the *Boston Guardian*

a. Why was Trotter such a vehement critic of Booker T. Washington?

b. Why are the Black press and Black leaders silent in response to Washington's statements praising Southern constitutions?

13. Race and the Southern Worker

a. What are the ironies and hypocrisies of Southern daily life identified by the author of "A Negro Woman Speaks"?

b. How does the author of "The Race Question a Class Question" support the argument that racial inequality is rooted in class conflict?

c. What are the White Southern workers' objections to socialism and how does the author of "The Race Question a Class Question" resolve these concerns?

d. What condition unites White and Black workers?

14. Ida B. Wells Barnett, Crusader for Justice

a. What profession did Wells-Barnett practice?

b. What was the true motivation for the rise of the lynch-law movement in the South?

c. What solution does Wells-Barnett propose to stop lynching and why?

15. William Edward Burghardt Du Bois

a. What field did Du Bois's research establish?

b. With which organizations and movement was he most closely associated?

c. How does Du Bois propose that the African American dilemma over racial and national identity be resolved?

d. Explain the significance of "double-consciousness."

16. The Niagara Movement, 1905

a. Why did some intellectuals and leaders join the Niagara Movement?

b. Identify three of the guiding principles of this movement.

Briefly explain how these principles are evident in the declaration of their demands and duties.

17. Hubert Henry Harrison, Black Revolutionary Nationalist
    a. What was Harrison's political philosophy?
    b. What lead Harrison to become a Black Nationalist?
    c. What are the differences between chattel slavery and what Harrison terms "wage slavery"?
    d. If class prejudice is the basis for race prejudice, why does upward economic mobility fail to alleviate racism?
    e. How does Harrison understand the relationship between class and race?

ESSAY QUESTIONS

1. How are religious themes used in the African American struggle for human rights in the United States? Draw examples from six of the excerpts in this section.

2. Review and comment on the arguments for the colonization project. What problems would colonization solve and what problems would it create?

3. Drawing on examples in the text as well as your own historical knowledge, discuss the relationship between Black participation in U.S. military actions and access to full citizenship for African Americans. What have been the arguments around this issue?

4. Compare and contrast the ideologies of integration and accommodation. How does each promote or prevent the realization of democracy and freedom in the United States?

5. Imagine that you are a newly emancipated person in the United States. What conditions would you face and which would be your greatest concerns? Explain why you would or would not become involved in Black Nationalism, the labor movement, the Tuskegee Institute, and the Niagara Movement.

6. Identify the organizations and movements in which African American women were most active. Why do you think that they gravitated toward these activities? How did their activism address their concerns and beliefs about the specific situation of Black women?

SUGGESTED RESEARCH TOPICS

1. The political history of the Reconstruction Era
2. The formation and development of White terrorist organizations and the history of lynch law in the United States
3. The historical relationship between racial oppression and the incarceration system
4. "Double-consciousness" and African American identity
5. The education of African Americans in the post–Civil War era

CLASSROOM EXERCISES

1. Facilitate a discussion examining students' understandings of the various definitions of democracy given by a number of people in the text. Then, have students write down their own definition of democracy (no more than a paragraph) and break up into pairs to discuss what they have written. Questions that they may ask each other might include how they came to have such a definition, how their understanding of democracy is evident in daily life, what aspects of society contradict their definition, and the relationship between democracy and economic conditions. Each student can then briefly present what she learned from the discussion.
2. Divide the class into two groups and stage a debate between those who argue that the race question is really a class question and those who argue that race is the most critical factor facing people of African descent in the United States.

MEDIA AND INTERNET RESOURCES

Films

In the White Man's Image (PBS, 1989), *One Woman, One Vote,* Vols. 1 & 2 (PBS, 1995), *I'll Make Me a World* (PBS, 1998), *The Black Press: Soldier's Without Words* (CA Newsreel, 1998), *Ethnic Notions* (CA Newsreel, 1989), *When Democracy Works* (Aubin Pictures)

Websites

"Picture History: Reconstruction Era"
   www.picturehistory.com/find/c/176/p/6/mcms.html

"An Outline of the Reconstruction Era"
  chnm.gmu.edu/courses//122/recon/reconframe.html
"Eras Relating to the Women's Movement"
  www.huntington.org/vfw/eras/index.html
"Black American Feminism: A Multidisciplinary Bibliography"
  www.library.ucsb.edu/blackfeminism
"Women and Social Movements in the United States: 1775–2000"
  womhist.binghamton.edu/index.html
"A Curriculum of United States Labor History for Teachers"
  www.kentlaw.edu/ilhs/curricul.htm
"Without Sanctuary: Photographs and Postcards of Lynching in America"
  www.journale.com/withoutsanctuary/main.html

Section Three

From Plantation to Ghetto

*The Great Migration, Harlem Renaissance,
and World War, 1915–1954*

KEY POINTS

- Jim Crow segregation was the general political reality for African Americans during this period in which the governmental authorities of the United States denied full citizenship to racialized minorities. This state-sponsored racism was accompanied by and necessarily complicit with the terrorism inflicted upon African Americans by White racist mobs both in and outside of the South.
- The Great Migration entailed the movement of millions of African Americans from the South to the Northeast, Midwest, and Far West. This migration was motivated by economic factors such as the mechanization of agriculture, the decline of cotton farming, the presence of better paying industrial jobs in the North, and the racial and political persecution of the South. Many thriving Black urban centers were created as a result of this mass movement of the population.
- A political shift occurred in which the competing dominant political ideologies within the national Black community were no longer accommodationism versus integrationism, but integrationism and Black Nationalism. W. E. B. Du Bois continued to

21

lead the liberal integrationist movement and Marcus Garvey emerged as the principal spokesperson for Black Nationalism. After Booker T. Washington's death, the NAACP soon became the leading voice of the Black middle class, reflecting a philosophy of liberal integrationism. The liberal integrationists were challenged however by Black Nationalism, represented by Marcus Garvey and the newly emerging radicalism of Black socialists such as A. Philip Randolph and Black activists in the Communist Party.

- With Garvey's imprisonment and the decline of the Universal Negro Improvement Association (UNIA) in the late 1920s, and the inadequacy of the NAACP in addressing the crisis precipitated by the Great Depression, a third political route that combined race militancy and class struggle emerged. The radical workers, intellectuals, leaders, organizers, and organizations promoted transformationism and advocated for the dismantling of institutional racism, the democratization of the U.S. state, the fundamental redistribution of wealth, and the elimination of all social manifestations of race and gender inequality.

- World War II, which gave way to the Cold War, dealt a debilitating blow to the American Left as millions of radical workers, intellectuals, and artists were expelled from unions, dismissed from educational institutions, imprisoned, and forbidden to travel.

COMPREHENSION AND THOUGHT QUESTIONS

1. Black Conflict over World War I
   a. What were the two conflicting interpretations of World War I?
   b. Why does Harrison criticize Du Bois's articulation of the position that African Americans should take regarding the war?
   c. Why do you think Du Bois encouraged African Americans to support the war?
2. "If We Must Die," Claude McKay, 1919
   a. What inspired much of McKay's poetry and essays?
   b. How would you describe the mood of "If We Must Die"?

   c. How does this poem address the conditions faced by African Americas in the beginning of the twentieth century?

   d. Do you find this poem to be powerful? Why or why not?

3. Black Bolsheviks: Cyril V. Briggs and Claude McKay

   a. What organization did Briggs organize and what was its primary goal?

   b. Why do you think members of this organization were critical of the NAACP and the concept of the "talented tenth"?

   c. According to Briggs, what are the manifestation and consequences of racism in the labor movement?

   d. What is the relationship between the Great Migration and the rise of the Black Left?

   e. Why does McKay advocate for the dissemination of propaganda on African American grievances?

   f. Why do you think McKay went to Russia? Explain why he compares the position of African Americans and that of the lower classes and minorities of the Old Russia.

4. Marcus Garvey and the Universal Negro Improvement Association

   a. What African American leader inspired Garvey and why?

   b. As an international movement, the UNIA was based in what areas of the world? Why do you think it was an international movement?

   c. What problems did the Garvey movement seek to address?

   d. According to Garvey, what is responsible for race prejudice?

   e. What sources of division within the Black race does Garvey identify?

5. "Women as Leaders," Amy Euphemia Jacques Garvey, 1925

   a. What was Amy Garvey's role in the Garvey movement?

   b. What is Garvey's vision of women's place in society?

   c. To what does she attribute the differing levels of achievement of Black and White women?

6. Langston Hughes and the Harlem Renaissance

   a. What project were writers, artist, and musicians in Harlem attempting to undertake?

   b. What themes does Langston Hughes explore in his work?

   c. According to Hughes, why would it be difficult for a middle-class Black artist to interest him/herself in Black subjects?

     d. What is essential for a truly great artist?

     e. Do you agree with Hughes's characterization of the "common element"? Why or why not?

     f. Summarize Hughes's explanation of the predicament of the Negro artist.

     g. What evidence does Hughes provide to support his claim that the economic color line is more predominant and severe than the social or political one?

7. "The Negro Woman and the Ballot," Alice Moore Dunbar-Nelson, 1927

     a. In which professions did Dunbar-Nelson work?

     b. What do the arguments used by women in their struggle for the right to vote reveal about gender relations?

     c. On what issues was the vote of African American women particularly influential?

     d. How can African American women better use their vote according to Dunbar-Nelson?

8. James Weldon Johnson and Harlem in the 1920s

     a. What were two of James Weldon Johnson's greatest accomplishments?

     b. What motivated African Americans to move to different parts of the city?

     c. What were the mechanisms of residential segregation in New York described by Johnson?

     d. What does Johnson predict regarding the fate of Harlem? Why does he believe that African Americans are less economically threatened in Harlem?

9. Black Workers in the Great Depression

     a. What was the unemployment rate for African Americans in the labor force during the Great Depression? How do you think that this affected daily life in a community such as Harlem?

     b. What was the cause of bitterness between Black and White workers?

     c. What does Harris suggest must happen in order to overcome obstacles obstructing the unification of Black and White labor?

10. The Scottsboro Trials, 1930s

     a. Of what crime were the "Scottsboro Boys" accused?

     b. What is the significance of the Scottsboro trial?

    c. Towards what audience or audiences do you think the Scottsboro Boys' appeal is directed? Why?

11. "You Cannot Kill the Working Class," Angelo Herndon, 1933
    a. What was Herndon's political ideology? Why was he arrested?
    b. What was so momentous about the 1932 demonstration at the Atlanta courthouse building?
    c. Explain why Herndon claims that there would still be a race question if there were no African Americans in the United States? Do you agree with him? Why or why not?
    d. How do you think Herndon's personal experiences shaped his political ideology and work?

12. Hosea Hudson, Black Communist Activist
    a. Why did the Communist Party appeal to Hudson?
    b. What means did companies and the state use to control workers?

13. "Breaking the Bars to Brotherhood," Mary McCleod Bethune, 1935
    a. With what organizations is Bethune associated?
    b. What does Bethune fear will happen to the Black man in America and why?
    c. Why do you think Bethune states that "the creed of freedom has not yet been written"?

14. Adam Clayton Powell, Jr., and the Fight for Black Employment in Harlem
    a. What campaign did Powell lead during the Depression?
    b. What did this campaign use as leverage to force businesses to end discriminatory hiring policies?

15. Black Women Workers during the Great Depression
    a. How did the exploitation of labor in the cotton industry affect women?
    b. Why did landlords let farms to sharecroppers with the largest families?
    c. How would you describe the relationship between the sharecroppers' families and the landowners' families?
    d. How do the experiences of Naomi Ward speak to the experience of oppression on the basis of class, race, and gender?

16. Southern Negro Youth Conference, 1939
    a. What were the goals of the participants in the Southern Negro Youth Conference?

26 *Study Guide*

b. Why was the growth of organized labor in the South considered a source of hope?
17. A. Philip Randolph and the Negro March on Washington Movement, 1941
    a. What organization did Randolph help to found?
    b. Why was a March on Washington Movement being planned in 1941?
    c. What was one of the dilemmas of the Black worker and how did Randolph propose that this dilemma could be solved?
    d. What was the dilemma faced by people of African descent that was highlighted during World War II?
    e. What parallel does Randolph draw between the United States and Germany?
18. Charles Hamilton Houston and the War Effort among African Americans, 1944
    a. What was Houston's contribution to the modern Civil Rights Movement?
    b. Why does the treatment of African Americans in the armed forces serve as a particularly powerful example in the struggle for desegregation?
    c. What does Houston claim to be the effect of U.S. racial segregation in the international community?
19. "An End to the Neglect of the Problems of the Negro Woman!" Claudia Jones, 1949
    a. Claudia Jones was involved in activities around what issues?
    b. Why was Jones expelled from the United States?
    c. According to Jones, why has there been an intensification of oppression of African American women?
    d. To what does Jones attribute the gulf that exists between African American and White death rates?
    e. How does Jones account for the subordination of African American women?
    f. Do Jones's examples of White chauvinism sufficiently explain African American women's insufficient participation in progressive organizations? Why or why not?
    g. How do Jones's ideas about the connections between gender, race, and class compare with analyses of gender by Anna Julia Cooper and Amy Jacques Garvey?
20. "The Negro Artist Looks Ahead," Paul Robeson, 1951
    a. Why was Robeson forbidden to travel in 1950?

b. How did Robeson combine his artistic talent with his social activism?

c. Why was it important to Robeson that non-elite people have access to art?

d. How did Robeson understand the role and responsibilities of the artist in public life?

21. Thurgood Marshall: The *Brown* Decision and the Struggle for School Desegregation

a. What is the importance of the *Brown* decision?

b. Why was Marshall's appointment to and presence on the U.S. Supreme Court significant?

c. What theory underlies racial segregation?

d. What examples of progress in the struggle to "remove race and cast from American life" does Marshall provide? How do you think that citing such examples helped to support Marshall's argument for full desegregation?

ESSAY QUESTIONS

1. How do artists and activists featured in this section address issues of class within the African American community? What are their commentaries, critiques, and recommendations?

2. Describe daily life under Jim Crow segregation from the perspective of both a Black and White person. In what ways did Jim Crow affect the lives of members in each group?

3. According to the material in this section, what was the impact of World War I on race relations in the United States?

4. Explain the relationship between racial injustice and economic exploitation as the authors in this section articulate it. How did the activism of groups and individuals seek to bring about racial equality and rights for working-class people?

5. What was the role of political organizing in addressing the problems of this era?

6. What conditions did World War II create or exacerbate that contributed to the emergence of the modern Civil Rights Movement?

7. The persecution of African American activists figures prominently in the struggle for equality and justice. Identify

instances of such persecution and explore their causes and consequences. What are the implications for U.S. democracy?

SUGGESTED RESEARCH TOPICS

1. The international labor movements of the early twentieth century
2. The impact of international migration on African American communities
3. Artists of the Harlem Renaissance
4. The rise and fall of the Universal Negro Improvement Association
5. The history of African American participation in World War I and World War II
6. The role of people from the Caribbean in the African American struggle
7. African Americans and the Communist Party

CLASSROOM EXERCISES

1. Have students locate and read interviews of people who lived through the Great Depression (or interview someone who themselves or whose parents lived during the Great Depression) and present their findings from this material to the class for discussion. Compare the experiences of interviewees based on their race, ethnicity, gender, and class backgrounds.
2. Students choose a writer or musician from the Harlem Renaissance and introduce this person to the class through both biographical information and a presentation of his or her work. For example, students may choose to recite poems by Langston Hughes, read an excerpt from one of Zora Neale Hurston's short stories, sing the Negro National Anthem by James Weldon Johnson, play a jazz document by a Renaissance musician, etc.

MEDIA AND INTERNET RESOURCES

Films

Against the Odds: Artists of the Harlem Renaissance (PBS), *Marcus Garvey: Look for Me in the Whirlwind* (PBS), *American Visions: Streamlines and*

Breadlines (PBS, 1997), *Second American Revolution,* Parts 1 & 2 (PBS, 1984), *Mood Indigo: Blacks and Whites—America Goes to War: The Home Front* (PBS, 1989), *A Lynching in Marion* (PBS, 1995), *Goin' To Chicago* (on the Great Migration, CA Newsreel, 1994), *Miles of Smiles/Years of Troubles* (on the Pullman Porters' Union, CA Newsreel, 1983); *Oh Freedom after While: The Missouri Sharecroppers' Strike of 1939* (CA Newsreel, 1999), *Trouble Behind* (CA Newsreel, 1990)

Websites

"African American Mosaic: A Library of Congress Resource Guide for the Study of Black History and Culture"
  www.loc.gov/exhibits/african/afam008.html
"African American Odyssey: A Quest for Full Citizenship"
  memory.loc.gov/ammem/aaohtml/exhibit/aoover.html
"The History of Jim Crow"
  jimcrowhistory.org/home.htm
"Virtual Jim Crow Museum"
  www.ferris.edu/news/jimcrow/index.htm
"Harlem 1900–1940: An African American Community"
  www.si.umich.CHICO/Harlem/index.html
"Harlem Renaissance: Life. Movement. Creativity. Revolution"
  www.nku.edu/~diesmanj/harlem.html
"The Jacob Lawrence Virtual Archive and Education Center"
  www.jacoblawrence.org

Section Four

~~~~~~~~~~~~~~~~~~~

We Shall Overcome: The Second Reconstruction, 1954–1975

KEY POINTS

- The 1954 *Brown vs. Board of Education* decision that determined racial segregation in public schools to be unlawful represented a legal victory in the broader campaign to dismantle racial segregation and thereby restructure social and political life in the United States.
- The successful desegregation of U.S. society represented by dramatic political victories must be considered in the larger context of the socioeconomic, cultural, and political metamorphosis of U.S. race relations. The significance of the Black presence in all aspects of American life from sports and art to politics and the economy received recognition and the destruction of legal segregation became inevitable.
- The victories of the Black Freedom Movement must also be considered in the context of the major shift in global politics that followed World War II. The United States and the Soviet Union emerged as the two competing superpowers and legal racial segregation discredited the United States' claim to be the bearer of democracy. As countries in Africa, Asia, and the Caribbean became newly decolonized nations, the United States sought to make them political and economic allies in the fight against communism and for global domination. The policy of legal White

supremacy was no longer tenable given these changing geopolitical issues.

- The Black Freedom Movement was a broad-based united front, which roughly consisted of those who wanted to assimilate within the system, those who were committed to social protest against the system, and those who sought to fundamentally transform the social and economic system associated with racial and gender oppression.
- As the legislative victories did not lead to fundamental transformation, the Black Power Movement replaced liberal integrationism as the dominant popular political ideology and discourse for African Americans for nearly a decade but never consolidated itself as a coherent social philosophy or strategy.

COMPREHENSION AND THOUGHT QUESTIONS

1. Rosa Parks, Jo Ann Robinson, and the Montgomery Bus Boycott, 1955–1956
   a. What was Jo Ann Robinson's role in the Montgomery Bus Boycott?
   b. What was the Women's Political Council? Why is it significant?
   c. What impact do you think that the existence of a reserved section for Whites only had on White bus passengers? Why?
   d. What factors do you think allowed the Boycott to be successful?
   e. What influence did the *Brown vs. Board* ruling have on the Montgomery Bus Boycott?
2. Roy Wilkins and the NAACP
   a. What accounted for the declining influence of Wilkins and the NAACP?
   b. To what does Wilkins attribute the increasing racial tension that followed the *Brown vs. Board* decision?
   c. What were White Citizens' Councils? Why do you think that Whites went to extreme measures to preserve segregation given that Blacks held relatively little power in the South?
   d. Why does Wilkins compare police action in Montgomery with Soviet Communism? Do you think that this comparison is valid?

3. The Southern Christian Leadership Conference (SCLC), 1957
   a. How was the SCLC different from the NAACP?
   b. What are the goals of the SCLC?
   c. How did Gandhi influence the SCLC?
   d. What were the obstacles that prevented African Americans in the South from voting and how did SCLC combat these obstacles?
   e. How does the SCLC define an "unjust law"? How would you define an "unjust law"?
   f. What impact does segregation have on Black and White people?
4. Student Nonviolent Coordinating Committee (SNCC) and the Sit-In Movement, 1960
   a. What was SNCC's primary focus?
   b. Who were the leaders associated with SNCC?
   c. What factors contributed to SNCC becoming more radical?
   d. Why was non-violence a powerful tool to end segregation?
   e. Do you think that this is an effective strategy in achieving fundamental social change? Why or why not?
5. Freedom Songs, 1960s
   a. What functions did freedom songs serve?
   b. What were the sources of freedom songs?
   c. In reading the lyrics of the two songs in this section, what do you think are the obstacles to freedom and how do people intend to combat them?
   d. Compare the ideas expressed in the freedom songs with the music and artistic expressions reflected in the Harlem Renaissance during the 1920s.
6. "We Need Group-Centered Leadership," Ella Baker
   a. In what positions did Ella Baker develop and utilize her skills as a community organizer and activist?
   b. What are the similarities between the reasons that she left the NAACP and the SCLC?
   c. How did the insistence on group-centered leadership echo the overall objectives of the Movement?
7. Martin Luther King, Jr., and Nonviolence, 1957 and 1963
   a. What international prize was King awarded in 1964?
   b. What were King's ethical and economic philosophies?
   c. What was King planning to launch at the time of his 1968 assassination?

    d. What examples exist that contradict King's characterization of the African American as patiently accepting injustice and exploitation prior to the 1950s?

    e. Why do you think that King linked the Black Movement in the United States with the international freedom struggle?

    f. Do you think that King's dream has been realized? Why or why not?

8. "The Revolution Is at Hand," John R. Lewis, 1963

    a. Why was Lewis's speech censored?

    b. What is the significance of the changes that were made (see footnotes)?

    c. In what ways does Lewis make a connection between economic justice and civil rights?

9. "The Salvation of American Negroes Lies in Socialism," W. E. B. Du Bois

    a. Why was Du Bois dismissed from the NAACP in the 1940s?

    b. How did Du Bois's political ideology change?

    c. What is the central idea of socialism?

    d. According to Du Bois, what is the relationship between the development of industry and the ruin of democracy?

    e. What is the program of the United States to which Du Bois refers on page 414? How has the majority of America been convinced to go along with this program?

    f. What is Du Bois's critique of American culture? Do you agree with it? Why or why not?

10. "The Special Plight and the Role of Black Women," Fannie Lou Hamer

    a. How do you think Hamer's personal background influenced her political activism?

    b. Why does Hamer say that she was "tickled" when people talked about integration?

    c. How does Hamer relate the struggle of Black women to that of White women?

    d. Explain the significance of "Up-South" and "Down-South."

11. "SNCC Position Paper: Women in the Movement," 1964

    a. What are examples of women being denied leadership positions and authority in the Movement?

    b. What parallel do the authors of this paper make between racial and gender subjugation? Do you think it is effective? Why or why not?

    c. What contradiction in the movement does this paper impli-
      cate?

12. Elijah Muhammad and the Nation of Islam
    a. How did Elijah Muhammad come to lead the Nation of
      Islam?
    b. What demands do members of the Nation of Islam make
      that are similar to other groups involved in the Freedom
      Movement? What is different?
    c. Why are members of the Nation of Islam against integra-
      tion?

13. Malcolm X and Revolutionary Black Nationalism
    a. Why did Malcolm X leave the Nation of Islam?
    b. In what way was Malcolm X's political and ideological per-
      spective changing at the time of his assassination?
    c. According to Malcolm, what unites Black people regardless
      of political ideology, religion, or class background?
    d. Why doesn't Malcolm consider himself to be an American?
      Do you agree with his argument? Why or why not?
    e. Why is Malcolm critical of the Democratic Party in particular
      and the U.S. government in general?
    f. Why does Malcolm agree to work on school desegregation
      despite his position on integration?
    g. How would you summarize the goals of the Organization for
      Afro-American Unity?

14. Black Power
    a. What brought about the emergence of the Black Power
      Movement?
    b. What is the significance of the Black Power slogan? Why did
      "Power" become a necessary part of Black Freedom Move-
      ment discourse?
    c. What are ways in which the vote can be used for social
      change?
    d. How is Ella Baker's philosophy of group-centered leadership
      evidenced in Carmichael's document?
    e. According to Carmichael, why is there a need for all-Black
      organizations in the Freedom Movement? Why must Blacks
      cut themselves off from Whites in order to proceed toward
      true liberation?
    f. What is Rustin's critique of Black Power? What contradic-
      tions does he point out?

g. What solution does Rustin offer to the problem of enacting true social change?

15. "CORE Endorses Black Power," Floyd McKissick, 1967
    a. What was "Soul City"? How did McKissick secure funding for this project?
    b. McKissick states that the belief in Black inferiority that allowed human slavery to occur has been quietly reinforced. Do you agree with this? Why or why not?
    c. What is to blame for the rebellions according to McKissick? Why?
    d. Why does McKissick resent "so-called Negro leaders"?

16. "To Atone for Our Sins and Errors in Vietnam," Martin Luther King, Jr., 1967
    a. In what ways were King's politics in the years just prior to his assassination more radical?
    b. What connection does King make between the war in Vietnam and the struggle he and others have been waging in the United States? Why does he say that the war is a cruel manipulation of the poor?
    c. What reasons does King provide to explain the distrust the Vietnamese have for the United States? Why does he provide this perspective?
    d. Some historians divide King's career into two phases: the early King who led desegregation campaigns and the later King who fought against war, poverty, and racism. When Americans today celebrate Dr. King's birthday, which King do they celebrate and why?

17. Huey P. Newton and the Black Panther Party for Self-Defense
    a. How did the Black Panther Party gain support within Black urban communities? Why did they patrol the streets of Oakland?
    b. What were the factors that lead to the decline of the Black Panther Party?
    c. What is the significance of forty acres and two mules?
    d. What problems do the rules of the Black Panther Party attempt to address?
    e. What is Newton's vision of the Black Panther Party? What are its most fundamental principles? Support your answer with examples from the text.

18. "The People Have to Have the Power," Fred Hampton
    a. What is the significance of the year 1967 to the Black Free-dom Movement?
    b. Why does Hampton relate racial and economic oppression?
    c. Many researchers state that the Chicago police were respon-sible for Hampton's murder. How did Hampton's ideas chal-lenge governmental and police authorities?
19. "I Am a Revolutionary Black Woman," Angela Y. Davis, 1970
    a. How did Davis come to be an international figure in the Black Freedom Movement?
    b. To which political and social ideologies has Davis contrib-uted?
    c. What reasons does Davis provide for being a Communist?
    d. According to Davis, what is the relationship between Black liberation and women's liberation?
    e. What does Davis believe to be the true reason that she was put on trial?
    f. How do Davis's ideas parallel those expressed by Claudia Jones?
20. "Our Thing Is DRUM!" The League of Revolutionary Black Workers
    a. What is the legacy of the League of Revolutionary Black Workers?
    b. How did the League understand the failures of the White labor movement? What reasons does the League give for its inadequacies?
    c. What are the crimes of U.S. imperialism according to the League? Do you believe these accusations have any validity? Why or why not?
    d. Comment on the League's short- and long-term objectives.
21. Attica: "The Fury of Those Who are Oppressed," 1971
    a. Why did the prisoners of Attica revolt?
    b. Why do you think that the inmates requested to be under federal jurisdiction?
    c. Do you think that the inmates' demands and proposals should have been considered? Why or why not?
22. The National Black Political Convention, Gary, Indiana, March 1972
    a. What were the objectives of the participants in the Gary Convention?

b. What are the crisis conditions to which the convention was responding?

c. What were the choices that Gary participants had with regards to social action? Why were these said to be the only "real choices"?

d. What do the authors of the document mean when they state that they "stand on the edge of history"? What is at stake and why?

23. "There Is No Revolution Without the People," Amiri Baraka, 1972

a. In what ways has Baraka combined his artistic talent with his political activism?

b. How does Baraka interpret the notion of "Back-to-Africa"?

c. What is the Congress of African People? How does Baraka propose it go about achieving its goals?

d. Why does Baraka emphasize the need for Pan-Africanist and Black Nationalist involvement in local politics?

e. Compare and contrast Baraka's views of the role of the artist with those of Paul Robeson's.

24. "My Sight Is Gone But My Vision Remains," Henry Winston

a. What is ironic about Winston's personal history?

b. What is the significance of the title of this section?

c. What did Winston believe were some of the actions and interests of U.S. imperialism? Why is this relevant to the Black Freedom Movement in the United States?

ESSAY QUESTIONS

1. The material from this as well as previous sections indicates that the relationship between individual states and the federal government has been critical to the African American struggle for rights. Identify examples and discuss the ways in which the balance (or imbalance) of power between state and federal governments has impacted the daily lives of African Americans.

2. What were some of the contradictions within the Black Freedom Movement? How do you think that they might have impacted the success of the Movement?

3. Both Martin Luther King, Jr., and Malcolm X were assassinated at a time when they began to develop a more international

perspective on the condition of African Americans. What are the implications of each leader's changing perspective?
4. What do authors in this section suggest about the possibilities of bridging class, gender, and color differences to achieve the goal of a just society?
5. What is the political, economic, and social philosophy of Black Nationalism? How does it contradict integrationism? Use excerpts from this section to argue for or against Black Nationalism as a solution to the problems that face people of African descent in the United States. How does what the editors refer to as "transformation" differ from both of these?
6. Drawing upon the material in this section, explain how the Cold War and the anti-Communist Movement in the United States affected the Black Freedom Movement.
7. What has been the role of the U.S. government in the repression of the Black Freedom Movement?

SUGGESTED RESEARCH TOPICS

1. Women of the modern Civil Rights Movement and the Black Power Movement
2. The relationship between international liberation movements and the Black Freedom Movement in the United States
3. The rise and fall of McCarthyism
4. COINTELPRO and the destruction of the Black Power Movement
5. The Black Power Movement and the arts
6. The Anti-War Movement

CLASSROOM EXERCISES

1. Have students develop questions and interview either a Vietnam veteran, a political activist from the period under consideration, or anyone who lived through the Civil Rights, Black Power, and Anti-War Movements and present the information that they learned to the class. Discuss how these personal experiences relate to the issues raised in this section.
2. Divide students into small groups and have them identify con-

temporary social problems and discuss the advantages and disadvantages of the various strategies of social action used during the period under consideration in this section in finding solutions to these problems. Write these problems and their solutions on the board/overhead.

MEDIA AND INTERNET RESOURCES

Films

Boycott (HBO), *Eyes on the Prize* Series (PBS, 1990), *Mississippi, America* (PBS, 1995), *Thurgood Marshall: Portrait of an American Hero* (PBS, 1985), *Fundi: the Story of Ella Baker* (1986), *Malcolm X* (Spike Lee), *Born on the Fourth of July, A. Philip Randolph: For Jobs and Freedom* (CA Newsreel, 1996), *At the River I Stand* (CA Newsreel, 1993), *Black Panther/ San Francisco State: On Strike* (CA Newsreel, 1969), *Freedom on My Mind* (CA Newsreel, 1994), *The Strange Demise of Jim Crow* (CA Newsreel, 1998), Emmet Till documentary (PBS, 2002)

Websites

"The Desegregation of the Armed Forces"
   www.trumanlibrary.org/whistlestop/study_collections/
   desegregation/large/desegregation.htm
"Civil Rights Movement Veterans"
   www.crmvet.org
"The African American Journey: The Modern Civil Rights Movement"
   www2.worldbook.com/features/
   features.asp?features = aajourney&page = html/bh00 5.html
"Civil Rights Movement"
   www.africana.com/Articles/to_199.htm
"Black Arts Movement"
   www.umich.edu/~eng499/
"COINTELPRO"
   www.icdc.com/~paulwolf/cointelpro/cointel.htm
"Buffalo Soldiers of the Vietnam War"
   personal.centenary.edu/~csnipe/final.html

Section Five

~~~~◆~~~~

The Future In The Present:
Contemporary African-American Thought,
1975 to the Present

KEY POINTS

- This period has witnessed a radical transformation in Black political movements and social thought due to fundamental changes within the United States and global economies. These changes include deindustrialization in advanced capitalist societies, the dismantling of the welfare state, the collapse of the Soviet Union and international Communist movement, and the rapid expansion of the prison-industrial complex.
- There has been a realignment of the ideological spectrum of Black political culture in which class stratification and internal polarization have been a dominant trend, effectively reducing the historical bonds of race-based solidarity. A central division among the integrationists has been between Black conservatives, who have been strongly promoted in the media, and the liberal integrationists, best exemplified by the Rainbow Coalition.
- Revolutionary Nationalism became largely marginalized as resurgence in conservative Black Nationalism, evidenced in the rise of Molefi Asante's Afrocentricity and the Nation of Islam under Louis Farrakhan, occurred.
- The Black radical agenda became increasingly advanced from the

vantage point of gender as Black feminists produced some of the most perceptive and critical analyses of conservative integrationists and nationalists. This tradition has also been evident in the successful anti-apartheid struggle, the changes in the AFL-CIO in which African Americans have played a major role, and the birth of the Black Radical Congress.

COMPREHENSION AND THOUGHT QUESTIONS

1. "We Would Have to Fight the World," Michele Wallace, 1975
   a. What does Wallace's 1975 book critique?
   b. Explain how Wallace's experiences in the Black Liberation Movement influenced her to become a feminist.
   c. Why do you think that Wallace was criticized for becoming a feminist?
   d. How does Wallace account for the absence of a Black Feminist Movement? Why do you think there has not been such a movement?
2. Combahee River Collective Statement, 1977
   a. What is the significance of the Combahee River Collective?
   b. According to this statement, what creates the conditions of Black women's lives?
   c. What factors contributed to the genesis of Black feminism?
   d. According to the Collective, why is feminism threatening to the majority of Black people? What are the differences between the responses of most Black women and men to Black feminism?
3. "Women in Prison: How We Are," Assata Shakur, 1978
   a. Why have some writers identified Assata Shakur as a political prisoner?
   b. How and why does Shakur problematize the social structure of the prison?
   c. What differences exist between female and male prisons? Why do you think this is so?
   d. What is the role of urbanization in the conditions of women in prison according to Shakur?
   e. Why does Shakur believe that it is imperative to the struggle to build a strong Black Women's Movement?
   f. Compare the conditions and issues confronted by Black

women in prison, according to Shakur, with the situation described by Attica prisoners in 1971.

4. "It's Our Turn," Harold Washington, 1983
   a. What is significant about Washington's mayoral career?
   b. How do the problems in Chicago that Washington identifies reflect both national and international economic changes?
   c. Why do you think Washington appealed to Chicagoans and how did he win the election?

5. "I Am Your Sister," Audre Lorde, 1984
   a. Explain Lorde's understanding of the function of oppressed groups in society.
   b. How and why is Lorde critical of the way difference is dealt with in U.S. society?
   c. Do you agree with Lorde's analysis of why the literature of women of color was not included in women's literature classes? Why or why not?
   d. Why does Lorde see the struggle as a "war against dehumanization"? What do you think that she means by this?
   e. What have been some of the consequences of misnaming the need for unity as a need for homogeneity?
   f. How does Lorde explain the treatment of Black lesbians? What do you think of this explanation?

6. "Shaping Feminist Theory," bell hooks, 1984
   a. What is hooks's critique of *The Feminine Mystique*?
   b. How does hooks account for many women's reluctance to join the women's movement?
   c. Why have middle-class White women been able to define the women's movement?
   d. On page 549, hooks states, "as long as [Black men and White women] or any group defines liberation as gaining social equality with ruling-class White men, they have a vested interest in the continued exploitation and oppression of others." Explain this statement. Do you agree? Why or why not?
   e. How do you think class privilege among Black women affects hooks's analysis?

7. The Movement against Apartheid: Jesse Jackson and Randall Robinson
   a. What acted as a catalyst for the Anti-Apartheid Movement?
   b. Do you agree with Jackson's argument that the United States

has a moral responsibility to assist in alleviating starvation and other tragedies in Africa? Why or why not?

    c. How did the United States support the political stability of the apartheid regime? What were the consequences of this support?

    d. How does the South African case exemplify the roles of the U.S. government as well as organized resistance in the international Black Freedom Movement?

    e. How does African American participation in the antiapartheid movement reflect a history of African American involvement with Africa?

8. "The Ghetto Underclass," William Julius Wilson, 1987

    a. What distinction does Wilson make between historic and contemporary discrimination? What role does discrimination play in accounting for conditions in Black urban communities?

    b. What impact did demographic change have on the condition of Black urban areas?

    c. According to Wilson, how has residential integration impacted Black communities?

    d. What relationship does Wilson make between economic opportunity and family stability?

    e. What nonracial solutions does Wilson suggest will address the problems of "the truly disadvantaged" and why?

    f. Would you classify Wilson's perspective as integrationist, nationalist, or transformationalist? Explain.

9. "Keep Hope Alive," Jesse Jackson, 1988

    a. Why do you think Jackson evokes the names and experiences of people who came before him in the Black Freedom Movement?

    b. Upon what common ground does Jackson suggest that the Rainbow Coalition stands?

    c. Explain Jackson's critique of Reaganomics.

    d. How does Jackson use his personal history to support his political message?

    e. Compare the issues raised in Jackson's 1988 address with the issues cited in the Black Agenda at the 1972 Gary Convention.

10. "Afrocentricity," Molefi Asante, 1991

    a. In what arena has Asante's theory of Afrocentricity been influential?

b. What are the differences between Afrocentricity and Euro-centricity? Why does Asante suggest that African American children in particular will benefit from an Afrocentric education?

c. What is multicultural education and how does Asante envision it to relate to Afrocentricity?

d. Do you agree with Asante that the United States would be a different nation today if students had received an Afrocentric education? Why or why not?

e. How do Asante's ideas about Afrocentricity compare with the ideas of earlier Black Nationalists?

11. The Anita Hill–Clarence Thomas Controversy, 1991

a. What does the nomination and appointment of Clarence Thomas as a replacement for Thurgood Marshall reveal about the U.S. political climate and specifically, Black political culture?

b. How is sexual harassment an issue of both gender and race?

c. Why does Jordan believe that Anita Hill's experience exemplifies the "traditional abusive loneliness of Black women in this savage society"?

12. "Race Matters," Cornel West, 1991

a. What does West mean when he refers to the "structural character of culture"?

b. Why does West call attention to the emotional, psychological, and spiritual state of much of Black America? What do you think this adds to discussions about the plight of African Americans?

c. Do you agree with West's critiques of liberal structuralists and conservative behaviorists? Why or why not?

d. How does West account for the growth in nihilism in Black America? Assuming that you agree with his assessment, what factors do you think could account for the increasing power of the nihilistic threat?

e. What does West mean by "a politics of conversion"?

f. What are his critiques of integrationist and Black Nationalist strategies for change?

13. "Black Anti-Semitism," Henry Louis Gates, Jr., 1992

a. Why does Gates argue that Black anti-Semitism should not be dismissed as marginal?

b. Gates argues that an aspect of Black anti-Semitism rests on the notion that "culpability is heritable." What are the implications of his critique for past and present campaigns for reparations?

    c. To what does Gates attribute the rise in Black anti-Semitism?

    d. Why is Gates so strongly opposed to what he refers to as an "isolationist" agenda?

14. "Crime—Causes and Cures," Jarvis Tyner, 1994
    a. To what does Tyner attribute the growth of crime?
    b. What is the role of the media in the crime issue? What is the role of the government?
    c. How does Tyner critique the way crime is constructed in U.S. society?
    d. According to Tyner, why haven't the death penalty, stiffer sentencing, and greater rates of incarceration solved the crime problem?

15. Louis Farrakhan: The Million Man March, 1995
    a. What is the significance of the Million Man March?
    b. Why does Farrakhan insist that Black men join religious organizations?
    c. Why do you think that the Nation of Islam was so successful in organizing the Million Man March?
    d. Many observers sharply criticized the Million Man March for its exclusion of women and emphasis on patriarchy. Discuss.

16. "A Voice From Death Row," Mumia Abu-Jamal
    a. Why is Jamal identified as a political prisoner?
    b. What is Jamal's critique of capital punishment?

17. "Let Justice Roll Down Like Waters," African American Prisoners in Sing Sing, 1998
    a. As of 2003, there were over two million Americans incarcerated in prisons and jails throughout the country. What role have prisons come to play in American society?
    b. What is identified as unjust about the criminal justice system?
    c. How do you think that the rise in incarceration impacts daily life in the larger society?
    d. What explanation is provided for the eradication of post-secondary education from prisons? Do you agree with these arguments? Why or why not?

18. Black Radical Congress, 1998
    a. What types of activists are involved in the Black Radical Congress (BRC)?

b. What documents inspired the BRC's Freedom Agenda and what does this indicate about its political agenda?

c. What problems within the Black Freedom Movement does the BRC's Principles of Unity seek to address?

d. Do you agree with the Freedom Agenda's statement regarding the conditions to which people are entitled? Why or why not?

ESSAY QUESTIONS

1. In this section, there are several writings by African American women. How do the experiences that they discuss broaden understandings and goals of the Black Freedom Movement? What are the implications of these experiences for the realization of democracy?

2. Audre Lorde emphasizes the importance of recognizing difference and challenging the notion that difference signifies deviance or inferiority. Has the struggle for freedom been hindered by the insistence on homogeneity and the perception of difference as threatening?

3. In what ways has the criminal justice system influenced changes in the Black Freedom Movement?

4. Both West and Asante point to culture as a critical factor to be considered in the plight of Black America. Compare and contrast the ways that each author views culture to play a role in the problems and solutions facing African Americans.

5. How are the ideologies of integrationism, Black Nationalism, and transformationalism evidenced in the works in this section? Do they appear to be in conflict? Why or why not?

6. Identify and examine a contemporary social problem that disproportionately impacts African Americans (e.g., poverty, prison industrial complex, teenage pregnancy, failing public schools, etc.) from a historical perspective. Trace the roots of both the problem and the activism that has attempted to combat it.

SUGGESTED RESEARCH TOPICS

1. Women political prisoners in the United States
2. The rise of the prison-industrial complex

3. The reparations movement
4. U.S. foreign policy in Africa, Latin America, and the Caribbean during the Reagan-Bush administration (1980–1992)
5. The evolution of Black feminist thought

CLASSROOM EXERCISES

1. Pair each student with a member of the opposite sex. Have all female students talk to their partner for five minutes, uninterrupted, about their thoughts on and experiences of gender. After the five minutes, have male students do the same. (The order of participation can be switched.) Then, have them remain in pairs and ask each other questions about what was said. Discuss the results of this exercise as a class, paying close attention to how race, ethnicity, class, and sexual orientation impact students' experiences of gender.
2. Have students watch television and read the newspaper for a week and pick out all stories that have to do with someone breaking the law. After a week, students bring in their findings and discuss the ways that the media portrays crime and criminality and the implications that this has for the struggle for justice, freedom, and equality.

MEDIA AND INTERNET RESOURCES

Films

Color Adjustment (CA Newsreel, 1991), *I Shall Not Be Removed: The Life of Marlon Riggs* (CA Newsreel, 1994), *The Body of a Poet: A Tribute to Audre Lorde* (Sonali Fernando, 1995), *Critical Resistance To the Prison Industrial Complex* (Video Activist Network, V.A.N.), *Race: The Power of an Illusion* (CA Newsreel, 2002), *Eyes of the Rainbow: Assata Shakur and Oya* (Gloria Rolando, Imagines del Caribe, 1997)

Websites

"The Prison Industrial Complex"
www.theatlantic.com/issues/98dec/prisons.htm

"Black American Feminism Bibliography"
   www.library.ecsb.edu/blackfeminism
"African American/Black/Womanist Feminism on the Web"
   www.library.wisc.edu/libraries/WomensStudies/fc/
   fcwedafran.htm
"Afrocentricity: Selected Publications"
   www.library.cornell.edu/africana/library/afrocentricity.htm
"Million Man March: Photographs"
   photo2.si.edu/mmm/mmm.html

Appendixes

Additional Sources for Research and Writing

The material in the appendixes was originally published in *The Rowman & Littlefield Guide to Writing with Sources,* written by James P. Davis.

Appendix A

Citation Styles and Style Manuals

If you are a beginning college writer and have not yet chosen a major, it doesn't make sense for you to purchase the standard style manual for every course you take in different fields. Most writing handbooks include enough information about the major style manuals to suffice in introductory classes. Once you are committed to a field of study, however, it is important for you to purchase the style manual that your professor or advisor recommends for that field. You will discover that many of the features of manuscript form, some of the features of writing style, and the format for both in-text citations and lists of references at the end of a work differ from one field to the next in significant ways. Learning to apply the guidelines for your field is part of learning the field. It might seem as if the differences from one field to the next are tiny, and they might seem arbitrary or merely a matter of a teacher's preference. But the guidelines are not, in fact, arbitrary. They reflect the values and methods of inquiry characteristic of the discipline to which they apply. For example, when formats in the social sciences seem to emphasize the year of publication, it makes sense because the recentness of information in the natural sciences typically matters more than it might in the humanities. If the natural sciences are meticulous about citing all the authors of a multi-author work, it makes sense because so many research projects involve collaborative or team efforts. You might not always know the reasons for features of the prescribed formats, but your work will appear more mature and professional if you care about and apply the guidelines in the appropriate style manual.

Here are some sample citations, included here only to illustrate a few of the differences among some prominent styles.

An article in a weekly magazine

MLA (*MLA Handbook for Writers of Research Papers*)
Strouse, Jean. "The Unknown J. P. Morgan." *The New Yorker* 29 March 1999: 66–79.

CMS (*Chicago Manual of Style*)
Strouse, Jean. "The Unknown J. P. Morgan." *The New Yorker*, 29 March 1999, 66–79.

CBE (*Scientific Style and Format*)
Strouse J. 1999 March 29. The unknown J. P. Morgan. New Yorker: 66–79.

APA (*Publication Manual of the American Psychological Association*)
Strouse, J. (1999, March 29). The Unknown J. P. Morgan. *The New Yorker*, 66–79.

APSA (*Style Manual for Political Science*)
Strouse, Jean. 1999. "The Unknown J. P. Morgan." *The New Yorker*, March 29: 66–79.

A book

MLA
Brooks, David. *Bobos in Paradise: The New Upper Class and How They Got There.* New York: Simon & Schuster, 2000.

CMS
Brooks, David. *Bobos in Paradise: The New Upper Class and How They Got There.* New York: Simon & Schuster, 2000.

CBE
Brooks D. 2000. *Bobos in paradise: the new upper class and how they got there.* New York: Simon & Schuster. 284 p.

APA
Brooks, D. (2000). *Bobos in Paradise: The New Upper Class and How They Got There.* New York: Simon & Schuster.

APSA

Brooks, David. 2000. *Bobos in Paradise: The New Upper Class and How They Got There.* New York: Simon & Schuster.

A website

MLA

Sierra Club Home page. Sierra Club. 6 August 2001 <http://_www .sierraclub.org/>.

CMS

Sierra Club. Sierra Club home page. 2001. <http://www.sierra club.org/> (6 August 2001).

CBE

Sierra Club. 2001. Sierra Club home page. <http://www.sierra club.org/>. Accessed 2001 Aug. 6.

APA

Sierra Club. (2001). Sierra Club Home page. Retrieved August 6, 2001 from the World Wide Web: http://www.sierraclub.org/

APSA

Sierra Club. 2001. Sierra Club Home Page. http://www.sierra club.org/ (accessed Aug. 6, 2001).

Appendix B

———✦———

Citing Internet and Other Electronic Sources

Citing paraphrased or quoted information from Internet sources requires some adaptation of your usual procedures. If you know the name of the author or of the organization, name it in your text as you introduce the material, mentioning the publication medium as you do so (website, CD-ROM, electronic journal, and so forth). If you are using a particular page from a website, place the title of the page in quotation marks in parentheses at the end of the sentence. Titles of pages or sections within sites are often quite long, and quoting them in your text in their entirety would be cumbersome. In such cases, you need to preserve the first word of the section name (to enable your readers to easily identify it among your list of works cited) and then use an abbreviated or shortened form that refers to the full citation at the end of the paper. Writing an abbreviated title isn't always a simple matter. For example, an underlined link on the NRDC main page is entitled "Protect the Arctic National Wildlife Refuge." The page itself, if you click on that link, is headed "Parks, Forests & Wildlands: Wilderness Preservation: In Brief: News" with another heading, "Arctic National Wildlife Refuge." In this case, the best thing might be simply to use "Arctic National Wildlife Refuge," as I do above, making certain that the actual full citation is clear in your list of works cited. The format for listing Web pages and sites will differ according to the appropriate style manual for your discipline. And, because the kinds of sources continue to evolve, most of the style manuals offer only provisional guidance and admit that the guidelines will be changing as the media evolve. But all the formats require that your final list include the author or organization (if known), the title of the page, the complete URL (Universal Resource Locator), the latest date that the page was updated (if known), and the date you actually consulted it.

It's not always easy to tell who the author is, and you might not find a date that the document was last revised. It's often tricky to decide whether a title should be presented as a part of a whole (and placed in quotation marks) or as a site on its own (and underlined or italicized). Given these uncertainties, it is doubly important to make certain that you do two things:

1. Type the complete URL with totally accurate transcription of every symbol (including slash marks and underlines) as it appears in the location box of your browser. If it is so long that you must break the line, do so only after one of the slash marks. The Modern Language Association (MLA) asks that you enclose the URL in angle brackets, < >, to clearly signify its status.
2. Make certain that you provide the date you consulted the site. Below are a few citations as they would appear in a list of works cited in MLA format.

A reference to a website:

Arctic Monitoring and Assessment Programme (AMAP) Homepage. March 1999. 9 August 2000 <http://www.grida.no/amap/>.

A reference to one page from a site:

Arctic Monitoring and Assessment Programme. "About AMAP." March 1999. 9 August 2000 <http://www.grida.no/amap/about.htm>.

A reference to one page from a site that does not provide the date of the last update:

Natural Resources Defense Council. "Arctic National Wildlife Refuge." 3 August 2000 <http://www.nrdc.org/land/wilderness/arctic.asp>.

OTHER ELECTRONIC SOURCES

Your computer might be linked to some databases to which your university or employer subscribes. Because you gain access to these databases with your Internet browser, they might seem like ordinary websites, but they are actually quite distinct from the Internet. One such database is Lexis-Nexis Academic Universe, frequently available on campuses. Lexis-Nexis offers searchable, computerized archives of published documents. This powerful—and expensive—service is a highly useful means of gaining access to electronic versions of materials originally published in a variety of media: newspapers, magazines, journals, newsletters, trade publications, and abstracts. Lexis-Nexis enables you to view and print information directly from your computer without the need to find the printed source in a library. It provides the actual written texts from the original sources but without the graphics, visual layout, and pagination of the originals. Generally believed to be reputably edited and reliable texts, the items found on Lexis-Nexis are really distinct versions of the original works. The service does provide the full publication information for the items, but it reformats the document in ways that do not enable you to tell on which page in the document a given sentence or paragraph appears. Because the item has been significantly reformatted from its original form, you must cite the version you consulted, indicating that the material was obtained through Lexis-Nexis. Presumably, the actual words have been transcribed accurately by the editors, but the authority for the accuracy of that transcription now resides at Lexis-Nexis. Your citation should indicate that the online service owns the version you consulted and that what you cite is at one stage of remove from the original printed text.

When consulting such an archive, you need to make yourself familiar with how it works—both with how the search engine enables you to make choices among dates and kinds of materials and with how the service organizes and labels the parts of the original citation. The author's name might be called the "byline"; the title of an article might be called the "headline." The services offer guidance and tips that enable you to figure out how the original citation would be reconstructed from what they provide, and most include a link to some sample citations following various formats. When you cite in your regular text a source obtained through one of these services, use the author's name (if available) or the title, as you would if you were

citing the original version. This reference, whether explicit or parenthetical, should clearly identify to which item in your list of works
cited the name refers. Unless the service provides the original page
numbers, you do not provide them. In your list of works cited, begin
by citing the work as you would the original, and then follow it by
noting the name of the online service, the name of the institution
that subscribed to that service and its location, the date you found the
source on the site, and the URL for the site in angle brackets. Consult
the appropriate style manual for your discipline for the exact way of
listing such a source. If you've found an item on a service such as
Lexis-Nexis and have not consulted the original version, you must
acknowledge the online source. Here are two examples in MLA format (the reviews I quote above).

Ansen, David et al. "Our Titanic Love Affair." Rev. of Titanic, dir.
James Cameron. Newsweek 23 Feb. 1998: 58. Lexis-Nexis Academic
Universe. Denison University, Granville, Ohio. 4 August 2000
<http://_web.lexis-nexis.com/universe/>.

Maslin, Janet. "A Spectacle as Sweeping as the Sea." Rev. of Titanic,
dir. James Cameron. New York Times 19 Dec. 1997, late ed.: E1.
Lexis-Nexis Academic Universe. Denison University, Granville,
Ohio. 4 August 2000 <http://web.lexis-nexis.com/universe/>.

Don't despair if at first all of these rules seem complicated. Much
of this material is probably review, and all of it will become second
nature to you with practice. The procedures for quoting and para-
phrasing are vitally important, even if they strike you at first as merely
cosmetic or surface details. Following these conventions will reassure
your readers that you are ethical, competent, and careful. And if all
of the papers you write are put in proper form before you turn them
in, you free your professor to comment on the substance of what you
say—things that probably both of you find more interesting. After all,
your professor has only a limited amount of space and time to devote
to commenting on your writing, and if your paper is in poor form,
you waste valuable time that could be spent on more interesting matters.

Keep this handbook and refer to it whenever your memory of these
conventions fades. In appendix D, I've provided a brief checklist. You
should consult it while revising papers that employ quoted or paraphrased material.

Appendix C

~~~~

Internet Resources in Related Disciplines

This section presents useful websites organized by disciplines within the humanities and social sciences. Some of these sites provide resources for research within a discipline, and some provide guides for writing papers and citing sources. Each discipline has its own resources and its own rules, so these sites provide an introduction to these resources and rules. They barely scratch the surface of what's available on the Internet, but they should provide a good start.

ANTHROPOLOGY

Anthropology in the News
Contains the latest findings throughout anthropology. Maintained by Texas A&M University.
http://www.tamu.edu/anthropology/news.html

Anthropology Resources on the Internet
General guide to online anthropology resources from around the world.
http://home.worldnet.fr/~clist/Anthro/index.html

Archaeology on the Net
General guide to archaeology resources on the Internet.
http://www.serve.com/archaeology/main.html

WWW Virtual Library: Anthropology
General anthropology resource with links for each subdiscipline
within anthropology.
http://vlib.anthrotech.com/

HISTORY

HISTORY
General resources for history organized by historical time period.
http://www.scholiast.org/history/

Horus' History Links
General resources for the history discipline. Maintained by the University of California, Riverside history faculty.
http://www.ucr.edu/h-gig/horuslinks.html

How to Read a Primary Source
Guide to reading and interpreting primary sources. Very helpful for
researchers.
http://www.bowdoin.edu/~prael/writing_guides/primary.htm

Welcome to History and Theory
This website and online journal is devoted to exploring the links
between philosophy and history.
http://www.historyandtheory.org/

Women's Biographies: Distinguished Women of Past and Present
This site is devoted to the history of women throughout the world.
http://www.DistinguishedWomen.com/

WWW Virtual Library for History
General resource with links to many history resources. Maintained by
the University of Kansas.
http://history.cc.ukans.edu/history/WWW_history_main.html

POLITICAL SCIENCE

Inter-University Consortium for Political and Social Research Website
This site contains social science data and resources for researchers.
http://www.icpsr.umich.edu/

Political Science Internet Resources

This site contains hundreds of links to political science resources. Organized by subdiscipline. Maintained by Western Connecticut State University.

http://www.wcsu.edu/socialsci/polscres.html

Social Science Research Resources

This site is a guide to social science research resources. Maintained by the University of Colorado.

http://socsci.colorado.edu/POLSCI/RES/research.html

WWW Resources for Political Scientists

This site contains links to political science resources organized by topic and type of resource. Maintained by the University of Colorado.

http://osiris.colorado.edu/POLSCI/links.html

SOCIOLOGY

American Sociological Association Manuscript Checklist

http://asanet.org/pubs/notice.pdf

Classical Sociological Theory

This site contains online texts of classical social thinkers. Maintained by the University of Chicago.

http://www.spc.uchicago.edu/ssr1/PRELIMS/theory.html

Research Methods Tutorials

Students at Cornell University have put together this site with lessons that include sampling, field research multivariate analysis, and analysis of variance techniques.

http://trochim.human.cornell.edu/tutorial/TUTORIAL.HTM

Social Science Hub

Excellent starting point for research. Comprehensive enough to include many of the major categories within the discipline.

http://www.sshub.com/

Sociology Online

This British site for all students of sociology, criminology, and social thought is full of information about both classical and contemporary thinkers.

http://www.sociologyonline.co.uk/

SocioSite
This site, maintained by the University of Amsterdam, provides a
global perspective on sociology with access to a number of European theorists.
http://www.pscw.uva.nl/sociosite/topics/sociologists.html

UCLA Statistics Textbook
This site provides a helpful statistics resource.
http://ebook.stat.ucla.edu/textbook/

Voice of the Shuttle: Cultural Studies Page
This site has references to a wide range of current sociological thinkers, many specifically oriented toward cultural theories.
http://vos.ucsb.edu/shuttle/cultural.html

Appendix D

Checklist for Quoting and Paraphrasing

1. Are all of your paragraphs developed adequately, with evidence for your argument or illustration of your complex ideas? Is the paragraph primarily your words, with quotations or paraphrased evidence serving only as supporting material? Do you provide too much information from sources, or too little?
2. If you have paraphrased, did you introduce the material from your source to indicate clearly what is from the source? Did you mention the author? Did you provide a note or a parenthetical citation of the source so that your readers would have all the information they need to locate the source and page from which the information comes?
3. Is the wording of paraphrased material entirely your own? Does it accurately reflect the viewpoint expressed in the original?
4. If you quote, have you introduced each passage, or does your context make it clear that the words are quoted from a source? Have you followed the quotation with a page number or with a note? Is each quoted passage introduced sufficiently so that quoted words fit together grammatically with your own, to ensure that your reader will understand the significance of the passage?
5. Are quoted words in proper form? Are they quoted accurately and marked by quotation marks? Have any added words or letters been placed in square brackets, and have deleted words been replaced by an ellipsis? Have you indicated the line breaks in quoted poetry with slash marks? Have you punctuated the quotations properly?

Appendix E

Table of Contents for the Textbook
Let Nobody Turn Us Around

Notes

Notes

Notes

Notes

Notes

Notes

Notes

Notes

Notes

Notes